Dru Yoga for all seasons

Dru Yoga
for all
seasons

*For Mansukh, our teacher, with great respect and appreciation
and for the Dru Yoga family world-wide, with our love.*

Surya Publishing
An imprint of Life Foundation Publications,
Nant Ffrancon, Bethesda, Bangor,
North Wales LL57 3LX, UK

Published by Surya Publishing 2003

Dru Yoga is a registered trademark

Designer: Caspar Graham

Commissioned photography: Michael Little Photography, Reigate

Printed and bound by Hamsey Lodge Press Ltd, Redhill

A catalogue record for this book is available from the British Library

ISBN 1-873606-28-1

Publisher's note:
This book is not a medical, therapeutic or remedial resource. If you are in any doubt about your health or medical
condition, please seek professional medical advice. The publishers, authors and photographers cannot accept
any responsibility for any injuries or damage incurred as a result of following any of the practices in this book.

Dru Yoga
for all
seasons

Padma McIntyre
& Helena Waters

contents

foreword

In all forms of yoga, but in particular in Dru Yoga, we learn that there is an innate connection between the cycles of nature and our state of well-being and health. We learn that certain exercises work best when they fit in with these cycles, and with the four seasons. All of the major texts devoted to the practice of yogic techniques emphasise the 'right time' or 'right place' to practise. Each season brings with it a sense of emotional energy, and the right exercises taught at that time have the effect of emphasising the positive aspects of that season. In this book, Dr Helena Waters and Padma McIntyre have created a flowing masterpiece, bringing together Dru Yoga programmes that will draw out the very best of each season for you.

I am often asked the question 'What is Dru Yoga?' as more and more people hear of it and want to know about it. I usually tell them that it is characterised by soft, flowing movements and postures, and that it is often called the 'yoga of the heart'. Other styles of yoga often begin with the physical discipline of stretching, toning, and coordinating the breath with movement, and then move on to inner work later. In Dru Yoga inner development is at the top of the agenda from the moment that you begin to practise it.

Helena and Padma have used their extensive knowledge of the principles of Dru Yoga to create these seasonally based Dru Yoga programmes. This is a rare treat in this day and age, as yoga is so often broken down into such small pieces that we can lose sight of the whole picture. The student of Dru Yoga soon finds that the macrocosmic view is in many ways more important than the detail (or microcosm), and the flow of energy/awareness in each posture is more defining than a description of some thing to be attained.

I have worked closely with both Helena and Padma for the last fifteen years and have seen the emergence of two very special people who are passionate about Dru Yoga, each in her own way. Padma is a master teacher and is well loved for her clarity, extensive knowledge, and insight into her students' needs Helena is also an enthusiastic educator who loves to see people rise to their highest potential through the transforming gift that Dru Yoga brings to them.

Very often we see pictures of people doing yoga in the gym, or on a yoga mat in a studio. If this book encourages you to take your Dru Yoga 'off the mat' and out into nature (maybe even with your shoes and socks off!), then Helena and Padma will have given you a gift that you can treasure for the rest of your life.

Chris Barrington

Director, International School of Dru Yoga

introduction

Everything changes and changes and changes.
In fact, change itself is the only changeless law.

Much of the stress that we experience in our daily lives is related to the amount of change that we have to cope with. Some people thrive on it and the adrenalin that is associated with it, while others experience it as painful and find the pressure difficult to cope with. Yoga gives us tools and techniques for coping with change and for learning how to flow with it, rather than resisting it.

Change is occurring all the time in the natural world and the answers to many of life's mysteries become clear when we realise that we too are part of the cycles of change that are happening around us. To see it, we just need to take time to enquire. Often we just need to look at life in a different way for an obvious order and simplicity to reveal itself.

In ancient times philosophers did not have the tools that modern science has given us. Instead they observed and learned to understand the relationship between human beings and the natural environment. They mapped out the rhythms of the energy systems that they believed connected everything in the universe. The ancient vedic physicians of India knew this, as did their peers in China.

In particular, they found that the seasons of nature provided analogies for understanding the growth and cycles of all things. This is true for our human life cycle as well. In many ways we also experience 'seasons of our lives' that may last for many years.

Most of us are naturally in tune with the rhythms of the seasons, even to the point of knowing intuitively when the seasons have changed. It may be a particular smell, a change in light or just a feeling. By embracing the changes and preparing for each season with clarity, discrimination and wisdom, we can learn to honour our body's changing needs as well.

Adaptation happens effortlessly in nature. The seasons epitomise the perfection of change and offer us wonderful examples of how to flow and be in the moment and of how to make change work for us and not against us.

In this book we offer you a series of four different Dru Yoga home programmes, one for each season. Each is designed to help you attune to the specific features of the relevant season. In addition to optimising the unique aspects of each season, each programme will incorporate practices to prepare you for the transition from one season to the next.

Although the practices are suggested for a particular season, there may be occasions when you want to capture the energy of a season regardless of the time of year or where you are in the world.

Most of the time we live our lives unaware of our unique, yet integral place in nature. The loss of awareness of this connection with all of life leads us to a sense of separation. It is this experience of separation that underlies every individual's search for happiness. The practice of yoga helps us to reconnect with our wholeness and our place of belonging.

In yogic philosophy our body energy is often described as being arranged on five levels. Dru Yoga encourages us to attend consciously to these different layers of our existence. In this way we can more effectively use our physical body and breath to control our mind and emotions, so that they become our servants rather than our masters. The creative power of our mind becomes available to us and we are able to realise the truth of who we are. We move from believing that we are small and insignificant, totally caught up in the endless cycle of living, to realising that we are noble and majestic beings, quite unique and with something special to give to life.

about this book

This book is written as an instruction guide for those wanting to establish a home yoga practice. It is suitable for beginners as well as those who already have some experience of yoga. It can also be used as a teaching guide by yoga teachers to add variety and freshness to their classes.

If you are interested in knowing about the unique features of Dru Yoga, then make sure you read the chapter 'About Dru Yoga'.

Many people enjoy doing yoga in a class, but if you would like to incorporate yoga into your life at a deeper level, then it is important to develop your own personal practice. We offer guidance in establishing a personal practice in the 'Getting Started' chapter.

If you are new to yoga, we invite you to begin with the 'Getting Started' chapter. If you already attend a class or have some yoga experience, you may wish to start with the practice for the current season.

All of the sequences and postures are well illustrated with clear, simple instructions. When you are first learning a posture or sequence, read the instructions through several times and study the pictures. You might find it helpful to work with a friend who can read the instructions out to you.

We suggest that you start by mastering the movements first and then add the recommended techniques for deepening your experience of the practice (in blue print). We also offer modifications of the postures and sequences so that most people are able to achieve them (in green print), along with any precautions you should take when doing the movements (in red print).

We use the *sanskrit* name for all the traditional yoga postures as well as the common popular name. There is a glossary of Sanskrit terms at the back of the book.

For each home programme we use the same activation, energy block release sequence and foundation posture (*tadasana*). In addition there is a specific posture, Dru sequence and *mudra* for each season.

It is important to complete each session with a relaxation.

If you prefer to follow the yoga programme by listening to instructions, you may wish to use the CDs which are available – one for each season. They are listed at the back of the book.

Please note that the postures and sequences are not restricted to particular seasons. We suggest that you work with the home programmes, not only during the relevant season, but at any time that you might like to enhance the qualities associated with that season.

The final chapter of the book offers some insights into the moral and ethical guidelines traditionally followed by those wishing to deepen their experience of yoga by living a yogic lifestyle.

If you would like to discover more about Dru Yoga you will find useful addresses for finding a Dru Yoga class or training course, and also details of other Dru Yoga products, at the back of the book.

about dru yoga

The way the body moves helps us to discover how life moves.
We realise that nothing exists in a state of rigidity.
Everything is in a state of flux. All we have to do is to have enough confidence,
enough love and enough courage to move with the changeless flow of life.
Within this flow we begin to find a sense of meaning to life, a sense of purpose
and an unshakeable discovery that we can achieve anything!

Mansukh Patel, founder of The International School of Dru Yoga

what is dru yoga?

Dru Yoga is a synthesis of ancient methods which are now being presented to the modern world, offering a unique perspective on yoga practices. It has developed into a powerful series of sequences, postures and visualisations which are capable of transforming health and well-being by balancing the energies of body, heart and mind.

When Swami Vivekenanda first introduced yoga to the West early in the 20th century he presented a style and form of yoga which was totally appropriate for that age. He recommended the practice of 'sitting still' within each posture by holding it, while at the same time focusing internally rather than externally. This style of yoga practice helped to cultivate inner strength as well as physical grace and poise.

More than one hundred years have passed since then and our needs are very different. With the rapid rate of technological advance, we find ourselves constantly bombarded with stimuli, fitting more into every day and living our lives at an ever faster pace. With such a lifestyle, moments for stillness and quiet reflection are very rare. A different form of yoga is now needed to enable us to withdraw ourselves from such 'busyness' and constant pressure. Dru Yoga is a style of yoga that leads us to stillness through movement, whilst at the same time calming the mind from its scattered focus into a laser beam of concentration.

The word Dru comes from the Sanskrit *dhruva*, meaning still and unchanging. Historically, *Dhruva* is the name given to the North Star, which remains fixed while all other stars appear to move around it. When practising Dru Yoga awareness is directed to that place inside ourselves, called the *Dhruvakasha*, which is still and spacious. This is the place where we are able to retain our inner tranquillity and strength no matter what is happening in our lives. It is like being in the eye of a hurricane, while the winds of life blow all around us.

It is in this place of stillness that we become aware of the various levels of our being – physical, mental, emotional and spiritual. This awareness allows us to heal and to integrate those parts of ourselves which we may have neglected or which may have become fragmented.

Stress-induced conditions can be tackled at a very deep level with Dru Yoga because of its 'soft body' approach and resulting conscious relaxation. Because of the interconnectedness of the emotions, body and mind, changing any one of them has the power to change the others. For example, improved mobility in the spine or joints as a result of yoga movements or postures can result in the release of stored emotions from earlier traumas. Furthermore, if we are able to release these stored emotions, chronic pain and disease will often be resolved.

In yoga the heart centre is known as the centre of transformation. Dru Yoga is often called a 'yoga of the heart' because a major emphasis is on activating 'heart power'. Many of Dru Yoga's postures and sequences are designed to stimulate the nadis (energy pathways) around the heart centre. This is a key factor in its effectiveness as a therapy.

Another feature of Dru Yoga is its emphasis on a soft, gentle approach to the physical movements. They are performed slowly and with awareness, often with many repetitions of each movement. At first it may appear that you are not working your body deeply enough to impact on your physical health, especially if you are familiar with more dynamic exercise programmes. With more experience however, you will come to realise that you are actually working the body at deeper levels. As you soften and enter a deeper awareness you may find strength, both of mind and body, which you would not have previously believed possible.

koshas – the five layers of our being

In the yoga tradition it is said that, as a human being, we experience ourselves on five different energetic levels or layers which are called **koshas**. Each layer is in itself distinct, but is also connected to each of the others and each layer is home to a part of who we are. Everything we do affects each and every layer. The finest layers originate in spirit or soul and the densest layer manifests as the physical body.

This philosophy of layering is not unique to Dru Yoga and is described in many ancient yoga texts. However, by focusing awareness on each layer, the practice of Dru Yoga gives us mastery on all five levels simultaneously and so transformation takes place quickly. In fact, traumas and emotional distress rise like bubbles through the layers of our being, surfacing and being released through the physical body.

annamaya kosha

The first layer (*annamaya kosha*) represents the material world and the basic material that makes up and sustains the human body through which we act and experience the world.

pranamaya kosha

The second layer (*pranamaya kosha*) is that of vital energy or prana which supplies the physical body with the fuel it needs to act and it corresponds to our physiology.

manomaya kosha

The third layer (*manomaya kosha*) is where we experience our feelings and emotions and also those of other people!

विज्ञामाय कोश

vijnamaya kosha

The fourth layer (*vijnamaya kosha*) is the realm of thoughts and ideas and is the closest layer to our real Self. The way we think determines whether we accomplish what our real nature wants us to achieve.

अनन्दमाय कोश

anandamaya kosha

The deepest layer (*anandamaya kosha*) is the Self that sits in the centre of our being. It is where all things originate in our lives and it connects us to the 'oneness' of life.

Who we think we are and how we feel about life depends on which layer of ourselves we're identifying with. Our experience in the first four layers is constantly changing. Our health, our vitality, our emotions and our thoughts are all in a constant state of flux. The fifth layer, the layer of pure awareness, behaves differently from the others. It isn't affected by what goes on outside of us or what happens in our other four layers. Once accessed, it can bring balance, depth and direction to our lives.

A wise being once said that we spend all of our time trying to fill our lives with trivial things so that we do not have to look at ourselves. It is sad that in the western world this culture of 'spiritual deprivation' has become the accepted way of life. It is very easy to spend most of our time keeping very busy, rather than taking time to ask the deeper questions about ourselves.

Dru Yoga style and form

The aim of Dru Yoga is to move from a state of activity to one of dynamic stillness or Dhruva. As a result you will develop a much deeper awareness and understanding of your Self and your connection to the world around you.

The Dru Yoga form is very specific. It has five main stages – activation – energy block release – postures – sequences – relaxation. Each of these leads to a deeper level of awareness, relaxation and inner peace.

activation

There is an intricate network of energy pathways known as nadis, many of which are specifically connected with organs in the body, while others are related to functions and systems of the body. Stimulation of the energy pathways improves and regulates the energy flow within the whole body and prepares you for the movement work to follow.

Always begin a session with a comprehensive warm-up which will help you to reconnect with your body. Many people are more mentally than physically active during their working day and they often don't realise how stiff they have become. It is important to warm up your body before stretching because soft tissues relax and stretch more easily when they are warm.

All your body systems are activated by this process, which enhances circulation and increases your awareness of your physical body. In addition it helps you to access your vital force, or prana. Sometimes when you feel tired
it may be that much of your vital energy is simply lying dormant, stored within your organs, soft tissues and joints until you release it. Activations provide a fun and easy way of bringing it to the surface. It is especially important to awaken the energy system prior to performing the energy block release sequence.

energy block release (EBR)

We follow the activations with specific energy block release movements that systematically mobilise each of the joints and, most importantly, the spine. This releases tension from stiff muscles, resulting in the body 'softening' and allowing more energy to become available. These sequences, which are unique to Dru Yoga, make use of soft flowing movements, breath and hand gestures (mudras).

the importance of releasing blocked energy

As we have seen, as human beings we operate on many different and subtle levels called koshas. In our daily lives we become very proficient at moving between these different layers and at giving and receiving energy on all of these levels.

For example, when someone is angry with us, the energy of their anger not only finds a niche in our mind but also percolates to the other layers, starting with those layers that are closest to the mind and then spreading outwards. Firstly we may feel hurt and then we may actually sense it physically, as the energy reaches the body layer. At this level the energy might lodge in our joints, causing stiffness and aching. From the joints, if the energy is not discharged from our body, it will transfer to the muscles and from there into the internal organs. Once this happens the energy block becomes deep-seated and if it continues over a long period of time it creates 'dis-ease'.

To prevent unresolved emotional energy from moving inwards to the vital organs we must release it regularly. This is where the EBR sequences have a unique function. The gentle movements work with the joints and muscles in a subtle way, releasing energy and allowing it to flow back out into the external world again.

Similarly, negative thoughts and attitudes can lead to rigidity in our actions and behaviour patterns, creating impenetrable barriers and defences which inhibit our capacity to 'feel what we are really feeling'. This includes our capacity to feel love and joy as well as pain and sadness. Regular practise of an EBR sequence over a period of time softens and begins to melt such rigidity around the energy and emotional bodies.

The movements initially release energy at a physical level and then gradually at deeper levels, but when we add visualisation and affirmation as well, the whole process is vastly accelerated.

It is a process which allows us to detoxify from the inside out and at every level of our being. It is as if we need to clear the debris in order to clear our vision. When this happens our self-transformation is even more effective.

postures

Dru Yoga incorporates many of the traditional *hatha yoga* postures, but presents them in stages and with modifications so that they are achievable by everyone. In the home programmes in this book we move from the EBR sequence into the mountain posture (*tadasana*) which, as the foundation posture, helps us to focus and centre ourselves before moving into the posture for the season. Each posture is interspersed with a period of rest. A feeling of fulfilment and success can be experienced by all, regardless of their level of flexibility or physical ability.

Dru Yoga sequences

We have discovered that many people experience less resistance to gentle, flowing sequences than to stronger, more demanding postures. Sequences of movements, practised in synchrony with the breath and with special emphasis on softness in the joints, direct the body's own natural healing and empowering responses to where they are needed. The sequences are designed to enable people of all abilities to experience a sense of accomplishment and ease within their body, by selecting movements which are well within most people's range of mobility.

The result is like a lifestyle 'counter-posture' – the more we are able to relax and find inner quiet, the more we can counteract the demands of constantly busy and challenging lifestyles.

relaxation

In Dru Yoga, relaxation is placed at the top of the agenda and is part of every stage in the process. You are taught to soften your body and take your time – the benefits of any movements or postures are felt in the relaxation and not in the action itself. A Dru Yoga session ends with a complete deep relaxation and sometimes a short meditation.

deepening your practice

We would encourage you to progress at your own pace and to remain well within your range of competence. Start by learning the movements and sequences that are easier to perform. Once you feel confident with them, become more aware of your breathing. Breath awareness is an important element in deepening your practice. As you advance you will gradually become comfortable with slowing down some of the movements and learning to synchronise your breathing pattern with each movement. If you focus on co-ordinating the breath and the movement, your mind will begin to relax and become clear of worries, anxieties and unnecessary thoughts. As your mind relaxes you will find that you are able to take your awareness even more deeply into the movements and experience stillness within the motion.

Many of the sequences incorporate *mudras* (hand gestures) which act on the body's subtle energy systems to focus, direct, and retain awareness or energy. *Mudras* are safe, easy to learn and can help you to change the way you are feeling when you are familiar with how to use them.

To deepen your experience even more we use suitable visualisations, and sometimes affirmations, in order to create a richer, more transforming experience.

getting started

Establishing your own personal home yoga practice can be a very
different experience from attending a weekly yoga class. It may be
that you are unable to attend a class and you wish to take up a
yoga practice at home. Or you may already attend a class and
have decided that you would like to make yoga a greater part of
your life by developing your own personal daily yoga practice.

guidelines for practice

One of the reasons given for not practising yoga is not having enough time. There are many brief opportunities throughout our day when we can stretch or do a breathing technique. For example, whilst waiting for the kettle to boil, when waiting in a queue or even whilst having a shower! Ideally, it is best to set aside an amount of time during your day when you can practise. Traditionally this would be in the morning before entering into the rush of the day.

It is ideal if you are able to allocate a room, or a part of a room, in your home specially for your yoga practice. Create a welcoming atmosphere in your yoga area by lighting a candle and perhaps have some background music to help you to relax and enter into the practice session with awareness and a concentrated focus. This sacred space soon becomes a haven of peace and you will notice how much you look forward to spending time there. Set aside a time when you will not be interrupted so that you can enjoy your practice.

We recommend that, when it is practical, you practise Dru Yoga outside in nature as much as possible and with bare feet! This will be especially beneficial when working with the energy of the different seasons.

Traditionally Dru Yoga is practised wearing loose, comfortable clothes that allow you to move freely. You might like to work on a non-slip yoga mat for safety.

Wait at least two hours after a meal before doing yoga. Make sure that you drink plenty of water after your practice.

If you have any health problems seek medical advice. Dru Yoga is gentle and therapeutic and is presented with modifications so that it is accessible to most people. If you feel you have special needs, a qualified teacher will be able to help you with postures and sequences that will suit you. See the section at the end of the book 'Where to go from here'.

If you are new to yoga, it is best to start with some gentle activations and energy block release movements and later add the postures and other sequences. Always finish a session with a relaxation, even if only for a few minutes.

releasing emotions

Our experience of using yoga with trauma survivors confirms that emotions can be physically stored in the body. Yoga practice, and especially energy block release sequences stimulate the energy pathways throughout the body. These are closely interconnected with the physical, mental and emotional levels. Occasionally, as pockets of long-held emotional energy bubble to the surface to be released, strong emotions may be experienced during or after your yoga practice. Be reassured that this is natural and normal and indicates that you are successfully letting go of emotions that have been building up over a lifetime. In fact, one of the hallmarks of Dru Yoga is its ability to transform the energy of negative emotions, like anger and fear, into their positive counterparts of creativity and courage.

general safety considerations

- Back care: Whenever you begin to unroll from a standing forward bend position, contract your lower abdominal muscles and bend your knees to protect the muscles of your lower back. Forward bends are not suitable for anyone with an acute herniated intervertebral disc (slipped disc). An experienced Dru Yoga teacher can advise you on other appropriate exercises which will help.

- Care of the knees: Protect your knees from pressure against the floor by using a folded blanket as required.

- High or low blood pressure: If you have either of these conditions, you may experience dizziness when you come out of any inverted position where the hips are higher than the shoulders. If this occurs, stop and rest. Seek expert advice before continuing.

- High blood pressure: It requires an increased effort to circulate the blood when your arms are above your head. Be careful not to hold raised arm positions for too long and adjust the frequency and number of repetitions to suit your own needs.

- If you have difficulty standing for any length of time, make sure that you sit to do some of the movements

- If at any time you experience dizziness, discomfort or breathlessness, then stop and sit or lie down.

some key points to help you

- Do the movements slowly and with a flowing, continuous motion.

- Do not lock any joints or hold your limbs or body rigid.
  Keeping the joints free enables you to experience a deeper
  awareness of energy flow.

- Move so that each movement originates from the spine. In order
  to do this, you need to use your postural muscles, especially the
  abdominal muscles. So, whenever you move into a posture, ensure
  that you contract these muscles slightly. This will create a stable
  base from which to move. This is particularly important in twisting
  and bending movements.

- Balance is important, so ensure that you repeat movements
  on both sides.

- Working with awareness of your breath will deepen your experience
  and each movement can become a meditation in its own right. The
  basic breathing principle for all yoga movements is to breathe in as
  you raise any part of your body and to breathe out as you lower.

- Remember: 'no pain, no pain'...your practice should never
  cause you any pain – please do not overstretch or overexert.
  At all times, listen to your body and be gentle with yourself.

- Do your practice with a positive attitude towards yourself. Believe that your body is your temple, to be honoured, respected and loved. Listen to your body. It will 'speak' to you and guide you naturally.

- Above all, enjoy the entire process. Don't get so caught up in the detail that you lose the flow. Detail and accuracy come with practise and refinement.

Like water which can clearly
mirror the sky and the trees
only so long as its surface
is undisturbed, the mind
can only reflect the true
image of the Self when
it is tranquil and
wholly relaxed

Indra Devi

how to stand correctly

In Dru Yoga the basic standing position is in a narrow stance, with your feet apart and parallel and your knees slightly bent. This position allows a free flow of energy throughout the whole body and encourages your postural muscles to work as they are designed to. We refer to this as hip-width, which describes the distance between the outer (lateral) edges of your feet, which should be approximately the width of your hips. Unless otherwise directed, you should use this stance.

You may sometimes be asked to stand with your feet shoulder-width apart, so that the inner (medial) edges of your feet are in line with the corner of your shoulders.

Wider stance postures will be described in terms of the number of shoulder widths.

These are broad general guidelines and you may need to adjust the position of your feet until you feel comfortable within these ranges.

firm foundations

In this chapter we will explore in depth the four basic elements of the home programmes that we present in the following sections. These comprise the core components of the yoga practice. In later chapters we add postures, sequences and mudras specific to each season.

activations

Use these warm-up exercises to prepare your body for the movements that will follow. Start slowly and gradually build up the momentum of each exercise, allowing your body to warm up at its own rhythm and pace. Repeat each exercise until you start to feel your body loosening.

1. arm swings

Stand with your feet hip-width apart and your arms by your sides. Slowly swing your arms forwards and backwards. Bend your knees as your arms swing down and straighten them as they swing up. Continue in this way, breathing in as you reach upwards and out as you bend forwards and down.

Gradually increase the swing until your arms reach overhead on the upward swing and finish with your arms swinging up behind you at the end of the downward swing. Try to keep all your joints loose.

2. spinal twist

Separate your feet to shoulder width. Begin to twist
your body to the right and then to the left. Lead
the twist with your hips, allowing your body and
arms to follow. Let your arms swing loosely so that
they wrap around your body at the end of each
twist. Turn your head in the direction of the twist
and allow your arms to swing up higher with each
twist. To increase the twist you can come onto the ball of your left foot as you
twist to the right and onto the ball of your right foot as you twist to the left.

3. side to side swings

In an easy relaxed style swing your
arms from one side to the other in front
of your body. As your arms cross in front,
bend your knees a little and as they reach
up to the sides straighten up. Start fairly
gently and build up the momentum of
the swing. You can extend the swings by
separating your feet further and bending
your knees more as you go down.

4. spinal wave

With your feet hip-width apart, raise your arms sideways and up overhead as you breathe in. Fold forwards into a relaxed forward bend as you breathe out. Breathing in, slowly uncurl your body upwards, starting the movement from the base of your spine, with your head coming up last. As you return to the upright position, raise your arms sideways and up, stretching your entire body.

Repeat this spinal wave several times, moving slowly and with awareness of your spine unfolding in segments. As you uncurl upwards contract your lower abdominal muscles to assist with the extension of your spine. Keep your knees bent until your spine is nearly upright.

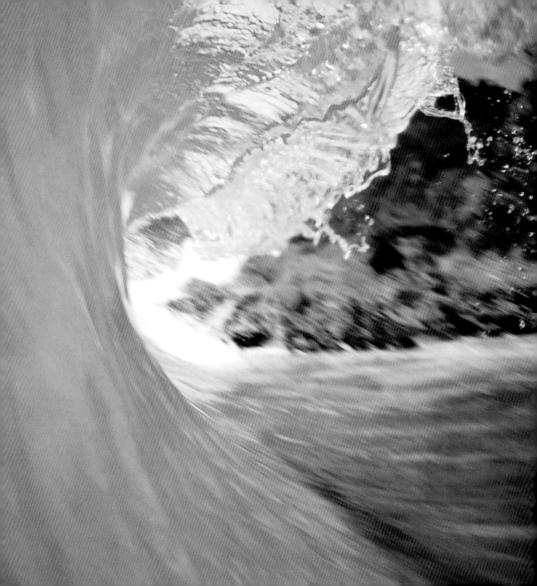

the mountain posture - tadasana

A mountain represents stability, strength and permanence. This very important posture can create stability and balance within us too.

This is also the posture from which all standing postures and sequences originate. It is important to stand in the posture with awareness and to focus on the various parts of yourself with the intention of bringing them into balance.

the posture

Stand with your feet parallel and hip-width apart, keeping your knees slightly bent. Tighten your pelvic area and draw in your lower abdomen. Open your chest by lifting your breast bone upwards. Allow your arms to hang loosely by your sides, shoulders relaxed.

Stretch your neck by tucking in your chin slightly. Lift the crown of your head upwards. With each inhalation feel as if you are lengthening and opening your spine.

Your legs should feel strong. Check that your weight is equally distributed over your feet. Feel your body relaxing and becoming still.

Once you have the correct posture you should experience a feeling of weightlessness and effortlessness. Focus upon the qualities of strength and stillness.

Note: It is important that none of your joints is locked, as this would block the free flow of energy throughout the body.

to deepen your experience

Once you experience a sense of grounding allow your awareness to move inwards. Sense the expanse of the earth beneath you, solid and firm. Feel the openness of the sky above. Visualise yourself standing in between heaven and earth, at the centre of creation. Imagine yourself bathed in the light flowing down from the heavens, and also bathed in the flow of the earth energies rising through your being towards the heavens.

At first this posture may appear deceptively simple. We would encourage you to explore and deepen your experience of it, especially by using the variations described for each season.

energy block release – awakening the heart

We will use this energy block release sequence as a foundation for the programmes for all seasons. It is known as the 'Heart Awakener' because of the way that it activates the energy pathways around the heart centre.

It can also be practised at any time to create lightness in your life or when you feel 'stuck' or trapped by your surroundings, job or relationships.

1. mountain posture

Stand in *tadasana* with your hands
in the prayer position, called *namaste*.

2. windmill scoop

As you breathe in, slowly raise your
hands up in front of your face and above
your head. Have your palms facing upwards, with
your elbows in front and slightly bent, so that your
arms are relaxed. Bend your knees slightly. Breathe
in and, as you breathe out, turn your body to the right
and lower your right arm backwards and
downwards, as if scooping up some water from beside your right knee.

As you breathe in, continue the arm movement, lifting high up in front
of your body to meet the left hand above your head. Repeat on the left.
Repeat this scooping movement several times on each side, finishing with
both arms overhead.

to deepen your experience

Visualise the sun above you, and your hands holding and distributing rays
of healing energy throughout your body, as you flow with this movement.

3. mirror twist

Lower your arms in front to shoulder height, palms facing away, fingers pointing upwards and elbows slightly bent. Keep your knees soft. Turn your right palm so that it is facing towards you. Keeping your left hand where it is, move your right arm around to the right as you twist your spine. Focus on the palm of your right hand, as if looking in a mirror. Pause, then slowly reverse the movement and come to face the front again. Reverse the position of your palms and repeat on the left side. Relax your arms down.

Once you have mastered the movements, incorporate the breath as follows – breathe out as you twist, hold as you pause in the extended position and breathe in as you return to the front.

4. heart breath

Keep both arms extended with your elbows slightly bent and your hands close to each other, palms facing you and fingertips nearly touching. Bend your knees a little more so that the energy flows up from the earth through your body to your heart. Bring both hands in towards your chest as you breathe in, palms facing you. Push them away from you as you breathe out, palms turned outwards. Bend your knees as you sink down during the exhalation, and rise slightly on each inhalation. Continue this flowing movement a few times, relaxing into the rhythm of your own breath. Finish by bringing your hands in front of your heart, with your palms close together but not touching.

to deepen your experience

Feel waves of calmness flooding through you as this part of the sequence soothes your nervous system and calms your mind. Focus on the space between your palms. Take a few moments to become aware of the energy flow between your hands.

5. ocean waves

As you breathe in, slowly move your hands
a little further apart and then, breathing out,
allow them to move towards each other again.
Continue gradually to increase the distance
between your palms, opening and closing
the gap between them in a rhythmical way,
breathing in as you expand and out as you
contract. Gradually decrease the gap between
your hands until, once more, your palms are
facing each other in front of your heart.

6. heaven and earth stretch

Breathe in, then separate your hands by moving your right hand
straight up and at the same time move your left hand down in the
opposite direction. At the end of the inhalation your right palm
should face up to the sky in line with your right shoulder and
your left palm should face down to the earth in line with your
left hip. Breathe out and allow both hands to reverse the
movement and return once more in front of your chest,
keeping a space between your palms. As you breathe in your
left hand rises upwards at the same time as your right hand
lowers down. Continue in this way, alternating between right
and left hands. Finish with your hands in front of your chest.

7. the archer

Adjust your feet to two shoulder-widths. Turn your right foot out 90° to the right and push your left heel back slightly so that your right heel is in line with the instep of your left foot. Imagine that you are an archer ready to draw your bow as follows:

Stretch your right hand out to the right with your palm pushing away and fingers pointing up. Bring your left hand in front of your chest, forming a *mudra* with the thumb up, forefinger and middle fingers extended and the ring and little fingers tucked into the palm of your hand.
(see over)

Stand with your weight balanced equally on both feet and your hips facing forwards. Breathe in and draw your left hand across your chest towards your left shoulder, keeping your arm at shoulder height. Feel the stretch between your arms as you create the necessary tension to release your arrow.

As you draw the bowstring towards your ear, transfer your weight onto your left foot, bending at the knee. Pause for a moment and visualise a goal you would like to achieve. Breathing out, release the arrow and let it fly towards its goal. As it does so, transfer your weight from the left leg onto the right leg, bending your right knee and turning your body to face the right. Gently sweep your arms down in front of your body, pivot your feet to face in the opposite direction and repeat on the other side.

8. forward bend

Relax your arms by your side, face forward again, and lower yourself down into a relaxed forward bend, with your knees soft. Allow your arms, shoulders and neck to relax in this inverted position.

9. runner into thunderbolt

Turn both feet to the right and come into the extended runner position by placing your left knee on the floor. Place your hands on either side of your right foot, checking that your knee is directly over your right ankle. As you breathe in, sweep your left arm back alongside your hip and then raise it up in an arc until it is slightly behind your head. Tighten your abdominal muscles to increase your stability. Pause and look up.

In the following dynamic thunderbolt movement, several movements happen simultaneously. As you breathe out, turn your hips to face forward and, at the same time, move your arm briskly forwards to a position slightly forward of your head. Look ahead and then lower your arm. Bring your weight onto your back leg, tuck your toes under and return to a relaxed forward bend position. Now repeat the runner and thunderbolt on the other side.

Return to the central forward bend position and draw your feet together.
Bend your knees and slowly begin to uncurl your spine one vertebra at
a time, remembering to contract your abdominal muscles. Work from
the base of your spine upwards, with your head
coming up last, finishing in the mountain posture.

to deepen your experience

On completing the sequence, raise your hands high above your head.
Visualise a warm shower of light within the palms of your hands. Draw this
light towards the crown of your head and let it enter you as your hands flow
down by your face to your heart centre. At the heart centre, pause, and bring
your hands into *namaste*. Take a few moments to savour the warm feeling in
the heart centre, like a soothing balm. Now is the perfect time to dedicate that
peaceful feeling to anyone you know who needs your love.

deep relaxation

No yoga practice is complete without spending some time in relaxation. It is during this time of release after physical movement that the innate healing response within your body re-establishes homoeostasis. This creates a sense of balance and well-being – physically, emotionally and mentally. This is why yoga's calming and healing effects are the perfect antidote to the stress that so many people experience daily.

Relaxation usually starts by relaxing the physical body to release tension, which then calms the mind and the emotions. Relaxation is not just 'doing nothing'. It needs a conscious effort to encourage your body to unwind and loosen up. It is a skill which can be easily learnt.

Choose somewhere quiet and ensure that you will not be interrupted. Your body temperature will drop as you relax, so cover yourself with a small blanket.

There are several positions which you can use for relaxation. The most beneficial posture is to lie flat on the floor on your back in the corpse posture (*savasana*).

savasana

Lie on your back and place your arms slightly away from your body with your palms facing up. Remove your glasses, jewellery, hair clips etc for comfort. Make sure that your feet are shoulder width apart. Before closing your eyes, raise your head to look at your toes and check that your body is lying straight and balanced. Adjust your position if necessary.

Lower your head and release any tension around your neck by gently rotating it from side to side before finally allowing it to rest in a central position.

Close your eyes. Focus on your breathing, allowing yourself to breathe naturally. Give yourself the sanction to be still and to relax. Aim to lie still for at least ten minutes – try not to move, as it is the stillness which will help your body to relax.

When coming up from your relaxation, first roll over onto one side, into the recovery position. Then, slowly push yourself up into a sitting position.

Guided relaxations are available on the CDs that accompany each session.

modifications

1. If you experience pain or tension in your lower back you can ease this
   by placing a bolster or rolled blanket under your knees. If your neck
   is uncomfortable, a small cushion can be placed under your head.

2. If you are pregnant you should avoid lying on your back after the
   first three months of your pregnancy. Lie on your side instead.

3. If you have a persistent cough or you have heart or lung problems
   you may prefer not to lie flat. Find a position that is comfortable for
   you, or sit on a chair.

4. It is also possible to do relaxation sitting in a chair. Ensure that
   your back is straight and that your feet touch the floor. You may need
   to support your lower back with a lumbar roll or a cushion. If your feet
   don't reach the floor create a platform of suitable height using yoga
   blocks or similar props.

the seasons of dru yoga

In the following four chapters we describe the seasonal variations of the foundation posture as well as a posture, Dru sequence and mudra for each season.

In the previous chapter we presented the activations, foundation posture, energy block release sequence and basic relaxation technique.

We hope that you enjoy combining these elements to develop your own yoga practice for each season.

spring

In spring the energy that has been accumulating beneath the ground in winter explodes above the ground. The qualities often associated with spring are – birth, rapid growth, vibrancy, vitality, creativity, renewal, fresh opportunities and new beginnings. There is a power and insistence that is associated with this new life. Spring is assertive.

A Dru Yoga practice designed to support and enhance the energy of springtime will be flowing and dynamic. The movements are selected specifically to help free up any stagnation and blockages of energy and to shed the 'holding' quality of the winter. This will enable you to discharge any excesses and detoxify. Creating a body which is fluid and adaptable to change will enable you to have a smooth transition into the summer months.

The tree posture is included here because it helps you to attune very closely with the upward-rising energy of the season.

Aerobic exercise is very important if we wish to cultivate and maintain a healthy heart. In spring we need to prepare for the fullness of the summer, which is a time when the heart can be under more stress, especially in hot weather. We recommend the Sun Sequence – a dynamic, flowing sequence which can be easily adapted to a pace and rhythm suitable for everyone.

The harmonisation mudra is selected for emotional balance, mental clarity and concentration at a time of rapid growth and change.

spring tadasana

We recommend this variation of *tadasana* in the spring because it is a perfect antidote for the stress and tension that mounts at this time of rapid change. It is particularly beneficial to use this posture for releasing tension whenever you feel stress accumulating.

You may also find it useful whenever you feel the need to balance your feelings and thoughts – 'to get your head and your heart back into balance'.

heart awareness breath

Stand in *tadasana* as described in the 'firm foundations' chapter.

Once you have established a firm, steady posture, and feel connected to your own 'inner roots', become aware of your breathing.

As you breathe in, let your focus rise from the earth up to your heart. Fill your lungs with a deep sense of calm, strength, courage and security. As you breathe out, take your awareness upwards towards the sky. Imagine any confusion or frustration in your life simply flowing out with the exhalation.

Breathe in, focus on your heart again, and imagine that you are filling up with fresh energy from the heavens. As you breathe out, take your awareness down into the earth. Visualise the earth absorbing any negative thoughts or feelings that you may have been experiencing and feel them being transformed into powerful, positive energy.

Repeat this cycle as frequently as you wish or until you feel mentally and emotionally balanced and able to withstand whatever storms may be happening around you.

the flowing tree posture – vrksasana

The balancing aspect of the tree pose stimulates your inner connection with the earth element, while the upwards and outwards movements of the arms stimulate the heart and lungs, creating the freedom and willingness to embrace life fully.

the posture

Stand in *tadasana*. Slowly transfer your weight onto your left leg. Breathing in, begin to raise your arms sideways and at the same time lift your right leg, bending the knee. Continue to raise your arms above your head and, as you complete the inhalation, put the palms of your hands together and rest the sole of your right foot on the inside of your left leg at whatever height is comfortable for you.

Breathe out and lower your hands down in front of your face to the level of your heart. Breathing in, rotate your wrists so that your fingers point forwards. Breathe out as you extend your arms forward at shoulder level.

Breathe in and open your arms sideways, drawing your hands apart, at the same time releasing your right foot. As you breathe out lower your arms to your sides and place your right foot back on the floor.

Repeat this sequence, raising your left leg this time.

Continue this flowing sequence a few more times on each side.

caution

If you have knee, hip, ankle or spine problems, do this posture carefully.
Keep both feet on the floor if you have had a hip replacement. If you have
osteoporosis, work against a wall or with a partner standing behind you.
Do not hold your arms above your head for longer than a few moments
if you have high blood pressure.

Stand Tall and Proud
Sink your roots deeply into the Earth
Reflect the light of a greater source
Think long term
Go out on a limb
Remember your place among all living beings
Embrace with joy the changing seasons
For each yields its own abundance
The Energy and Birth of Spring
The Growth and Contentment of Summer
The Wisdom to let go of leaves in the Fall
The Rest and Quiet Renewal of Winter

Enjoy the view!

Ilan Shamir, Advice From a Tree

the sun sequence – surya namaskara

In this sequence, start slowly, taking time to establish good balance
and correct posture. Work out how to make the transitions between the
movements, remembering that slight differences will apply for each individual
due to their unique body build. The whole body is exercised, improving the
elimination functions and enabling the body to detoxify more efficiently. The
sun sequence also stimulates the entire endocrine system, thus helping us
to maintain hormone balance.

There are many variations of the sun sequence.
This one is particularly suitable for beginners.

surya namaskara

1. Stand in *tadasana* with your hands in
the *namaste mudra* in front of your chest.

to deepen your experience

Take a few minutes to connect your whole being with the earth and
the heavens. Visualise an early morning sky. The sun is about to rise
over the horizon. Feel a sense of anticipation – the potential of the
day ahead lies dormant as you greet this fresh new dawn.

2. Breathe in, raise your hands up above your head, still in the praying hands position. Separate your hands, lean back slightly and look up.

As you exhale, bend forwards, and at the same time lower your arms down towards your legs, knees bent.

Begin to straighten up on an in-breath, contracting your abdominal muscles and moving your hands up the front of your body as you rise up. Stretch your arms up above your head and lean back slightly once again.

Repeat this curling and unrolling movement twice more, finishing in the forward bend.

3. Place your hands on the floor on either side of your feet. Taking the weight on your hands and left foot, stretch your right leg back as far as is comfortable, coming into the runner position. Check that your left knee is directly above the ankle. Breathe in and raise your arms upwards, opening them overhead. Breathe out, bend forward again towards your left thigh, swinging your arms down and behind your back. Repeat this movement twice more. Finish with your hands flat on the floor.

4. Taking your weight onto your hands,
step back with your left leg, into the inclined plane (push-up) position.
Contract your buttocks and your lower abdominal muscles. With your body
and legs in as straight a line as possible, slowly lower to lie flat on the floor.

modification: put your knees down first and then follow with the rest of the body.

Breathe in and raise your head and upper body off the ground. Make sure that
your navel remains in contact with the floor. This is the cobra posture. Breathe
out and gently lower to the ground again, tucking in your chin and elongating
your neck as you lower. Repeat this movement twice more, lifting your body a
little higher each time. The third time pause for a few moments in the cobra,
breathe normally and then lower down.

5. Tuck your toes under, go back into the inclined plane and, raising your hips into the air, move into the dog posture. Separate your feet to two shoulder widths, press your heels down and relax your head between your arms.

6. Bring your feet to hip width again and then step forward with your right leg, lowering the left knee to the ground and coming into the runner position once more. Breathe in and raise your arms up, as before. Breathe out as you lower over your right thigh. Repeat twice more. Finish with your hands flat on the floor on either side of your right foot.

7. Breathe in and bring your left leg forward to join the right, coming back into the forward bend pose. Breathe out and relax.

8. Breathe in, bend your knees, contract your lower abdominal muscles and slowly straighten your spine, starting from the base upwards. Continue the upwards movement, raising your arms into an overhead stretch. Breathe out and return to the relaxed forward bend. Repeat twice more. Finish in *tadasana*. Bring your hands into *namaste* and pause while you re-establish a regular breathing pattern.

Repeat the whole sequence, this time taking the left leg back into the runner pose first. This completes one round of the sun sequence.

caution

As this is a strenuous sequence, it may not be suitable for those with serious joint problems, heart disease or high or low blood pressure. Pregnant women should not do it, and during menstruation, women should omit the cobra and dog postures.

harmonisation mudra

This simple mudra, when used even for just a few minutes at a time, can help you to connect with the energy of the season so that you feel in tune and in harmony. It also helps to harmonise the right and left hemispheres of your brain so that at those times when you may be over-excited and agitated it induces relaxation and calmness. At other times, when you are feeling tired or lethargic, it helps to increase alertness, concentration and mental acuity.

Sit comfortably and start with your hands in the praying hands mudra in front of your chest. Open your hands out but keep your fingers and thumbs touching at the tips. Spread your fingers wide apart and create an open space in the centre between the palms. Keep the finger joints slightly bent.

When you feel comfortable holding the gesture, bring your hands nearer to you with your thumbs close to your chest. Relax your shoulders and hold the mudra for a few minutes, focusing on keeping a calm, smooth regular breathing pattern.

Depending on which you need, you can visualise and affirm either a process of relaxation or energisation.

If you need to become more still and quiet inside, focus on breathing in and out for an equal length of time.

If you need to raise your energy, focus on drawing energy into your body with every inhalation.

To release the mudra, return to the praying hands mudra. When you feel ready allow your hands to separate gently.

summer

activation

tadasana – eagle high

energy block release sequence

bridge posture

seat of compassion sequence

deep relaxation

lotus mudra

Summer is a time of fulfilment and fruition. In the long days there is radiance, warmth, exuberance, joyfulness and delight in the richness of the moment. The fire energy is rapid, random and rising. Passion is easily ignited, together with the enthusiasm and the 'high' that we experience when we know that everything is possible. It is a time of potential excess, of over-activity and of over-excitement.

The challenge in summer is to maintain equilibrium at a time when your energies can be easily dispersed. Faced with many choices and diverse activities demanding your time, energy and attention, you need to avoid over-commitment, exhaustion and burn-out. How successfully you negotiate this will determine how well you manage your emotions and your energy levels.

At this time it is important to develop your ability to concentrate which will enable you to remain balanced and inwardly calm and still.

The summer Dru Yoga programme lends itself well to practising outside. We highly recommend you perform the *tadasana* and visualisation standing barefoot on the earth. Practised in this way it is very grounding and creates a space from which you can experience more clarity and discrimination.

The bridge posture offers a very gentle inverted pose and backward bend. It helps to divert excess energy upwards towards the heart, bringing a sense of abundance and joy.

By opening the energy pathways around the heart, the Seat of Compassion sequence will help you to manage powerful summer emotions. You will be able to utilise the energy of these emotions more effectively and make considered choices rather than reacting to external events and circumstances.

The lotus mudra acts directly on energetic pathways around the heart and when practised regularly is particularly helpful in managing the emotions which express themselves in the summer.

summer tadasana

This variation of the mountain posture is recommended for the summer because it provides a wonderful way of keeping a balance between your plans and the practicalities of implementing them.

It can also be helpful for those times when you feel overwhelmed by life or when you are too close to an issue and need to rise above it in order to see it clearly.

eagle high

Spend several moments in tadasana, ensuring that your feet are well anchored to the earth and that your balance is steady.

Be aware of your chest gently rising and falling as you breathe in and out. When you feel warmth building in your chest, move on to the next stage.

With every inhalation feel as if your breath is rising up through an opening in the crown of your head. As you breathe out feel the breath dissolving into the space around you. With your feet firmly anchored in the earth and your awareness totally focused on your breathing imagine yourself soaring upwards into the space above you.

Repeat this at least five times, each time putting distance between you and your thoughts. With a renewed sense of freedom and a fresh perspective, bring your awareness once again to your feet, firm upon the earth like roots.

the bridge – setubandhasana

This posture, which is done as a flowing sequence (viṅyasa), involves a progressive lifting and lowering of the spinal vertebrae, moving from the base of the spine upwards. The intention is to move each individual vertebra, allowing the spinal energy to flow freely. The posture provides a powerful re-connection with the spine, which often becomes stressed during periods of over-activity.

This posture is ideal for the summer because it is calming and helps to free any energy blocks in the pelvic and abdominal cavities. This helps to maintain good functioning of the reproductive, digestive and elimination systems.

the posture

Lie on your back, with your knees bent and feet flat on the floor.

On an in-breath, raise your tail bone up off the floor. On an out-breath, lower it down again. Next, raise your sacrum and lowest lumbar vertebra (L5) and, as you breathe out, lower the vertebra and then the sacrum. Again raise the sacrum, L5 and L4 as you breathe in, lowering in reverse order as you breathe out. Continue in this way, working all the way up the spine as far as is comfortable. Finish in the starting position.

caution

It's important to keep your feet flat on the floor. Avoid turning them out sideways.

the seat of compassion sequence

1. lotus chair

Standing in *tadasana*, with your hands in *namaste*, inhale and slowly raise your arms up above your head until your palms meet. Breathe out and lower your hands towards the crown of your head. Adopt the lotus bud *mudra* at this point by creating a cupped space between your palms. Breathe in and slowly extend your hands upwards while your knees bend and you sink downwards from your hips. Open your hands into the lotus *mudra*, keeping a light contact between the heels of your hands and with your little fingers touching. Spread your fingers wide apart, as if they were petals opening to the sun. In this way continue to alternate between the opening and closing of the lotus *mudra* as you breathe in and out three more times, finishing with your hands overhead. See *lotus mudra* on p.101

2. charity pose

Separate your hands. Slowly lower your arms down to your sides and then bring your hands behind your back so that your palms meet, fingers facing downwards. Bring your shoulders and elbows back and turn your wrists so that your fingers point upwards along your spine. Raise these 'praying hands' up until they rest against your back between your shoulder blades or as high as is comfortable. Press your palms together strongly.

modification

If this position is uncomfortable, bring the right hand to hold the left elbow and the left hand to hold the right elbow.

Separate your feet to two shoulder widths apart, turn your right foot out to the right and push your left heel back slightly. Rotate your body towards the right, keeping your legs straight. Breathe in and arch your back slightly. As you breathe out, bend forward from your hips, keeping your back straight and right knee bent. Bend forward as far as comfortable. On the next in-breath, come up by gradually straightening your right knee and unrolling from the base of your spine, whilst transferring your weight onto your back leg. Arch back and continue to repeat this wave-like movement several times. Finally, separate your hands, place them on the floor and relax forward over your right leg, breathing naturally.

3. seat of compassion pose

Come into the runner position by bringing your left knee onto the floor. Check that your right knee is directly above your right ankle. Raise both arms in front of you to shoulder height, palms facing forward. Inhale and raise your left hand above your head.

As you exhale, start to turn your body slowly so that you can follow the movement of your hand with your eyes, and lower your left hand behind you to shoulder height. Breathe in and soften your shoulders and elbows, drawing your hands a little closer to your body. Breathe out and extend your arms out again, creating a wave-like movement with your arms. Breathe in and raise your left arm as you slowly turn your head to look forward. Breathe out, lower your arm and return to your original position, with both palms extended in front of you.

modification

The above arm movements may be difficult. An easier variation is to lower
your arm down and backwards as your head turns to look behind, then
down and forwards to return.

4. charity pose

Place both hands onto the floor in front and pause until you can establish your balance. Bring your hands off the floor and either take hold of your elbows or bring your hands into the prayer position behind your back once again. Keep your right knee bent as you gradually raise up from the base of your spine, bringing your body upright, raising your head last. Turn your feet to face forwards and bring them close together. Turn your hands so that your fingers point down.

Repeat with the opposite leg and arm.

8. Complete by standing in *tadasana* and bring your hands into *namaste*.

lotus mudra

The lotus is a pond flower, similar to the water lily. It is symbolic of our search to rise above the mundane aspects of life and to blossom into our full potential. No matter how 'muddy' or polluted our environment becomes we can, like the lotus, always rise upwards towards the light. The lotus has thick waxy leaves which allow water to roll off easily – in the same way we can allow life's challenges to roll off us without affecting our peace of mind.

Sit comfortably, holding the praying hands mudra in front of you. Bend your fingers slightly so that there is a space between your palms and let your thumbs come together in the centre. This resembles the flower in bud. As you breathe in separate your hands and stretch your fingers apart, but keep a light contact at the tips of the little fingers and the heels of the hands. Draw your hands in so that they are at heart level.

Allow your fingers to spread as wide apart as comfortable and create an open space between your palms. As you breathe out allow your fingers to curl slowly towards each other once more. With each inhalation open the petals of the lotus flower as described above and close them again as you exhale. Make sure that your shoulders are relaxed.

Repeat this several times, slowly allowing your focus to go inwards to the area of your heart.

Affirm several times:

> *I have the courage and strength to open and to unfold my full potential*

When you feel ready, bring your hands to the praying hands mudra and then gently separate them.

autumn

activation

tadasana – deep roots into the earth

energy block release sequence

rotated triangle posture

earth sequence

deep relaxation

mudra of letting go

The main energy of autumn is that of completion and the satisfaction of attainment. There is a stillness, serenity and gracefulness as we glide through this season of restrained energies. The image of a tall tree that has lost its leaves stretching between the heavens and the earth captures the dignity of the season.

The autumn Dru Yoga session is characterised by movements which help to release and resolve the past, eliminate what has not been useful and develop an inner focus. Autumn is a time when you reflect and contemplate on what has been worthwhile and meaningful, leading to greater clarity and purpose.

You may prefer less dynamic movements and this is reflected in the autumn programme.

The rotated triangle pose is included because it contains both forward bending movements and spinal twisting. Forward bends allow you to yield more easily, surrendering and letting go of whatever you no longer need to hold on to. The twisting movements allow you to view a situation from many different perspectives, revealing new insights and allowing you to learn from the past and leave it behind.

The Earth Sequence has a gentle pace and synchronises breath and movement. It also works on strengthening the legs and associated kidney energy, in preparation for the winter.

We chose the mudra of letting go for this season because it opens energy pathways that enable you to release unwanted emotions or uncomfortable memories, situations or habit patterns.

autumn tadasana

In autumn you deepen your experience of *tadasana* by focusing on being and feeling grounded. This variation is also useful when you need to strengthen your self-confidence or to feel more 'anchored'.

deep roots into the earth

Allow yourself to settle into *tadasana* for a few moments. Notice how you experience the posture and give your body, heart and mind permission to relax.

Become aware of your feet and the contact they make with the earth. Each time you breathe in, imagine strong roots spreading outwards and down from the soles of your feet into the earth below. As you breathe out imagine the roots taking hold. Hold your awareness at this place so that your next inhalation will allow the roots to extend deeper and wider.

Continue in this way for five or six breaths, visualising your roots spreading deep into the earth.

To complete the cycle, bring your attention to your whole body once more. With each inhalation draw your awareness up from the roots into your legs, pelvis, abdomen and chest. Focus on the warmth in the centre of your chest for a few more breaths. Acknowledge your innate power and strength as you affirm:

I am whole and complete exactly as I am now

the rotated triangle – parivritta trikonasana

the posture

Stand in *tadasana* and separate your legs two shoulder widths. Turn your right foot to the right and push your left heel back to the left. Still facing forwards, breathe in and raise your arms sideways to shoulder height.

Breathe out and lower your left arm, taking it past your left hip, whilst at the same time turning your body to face the right. As your left arm moves up to shoulder level in front, bring your right hand down and back towards your right hip.

Breathe in and stretch your left hand forwards. Breathe out, bend forward over your right leg and place your left hand on the floor by the outer edge of your right foot, keeping your knee soft.

Breathe normally and take time to feel balanced and steady.

Inhale and unfold your right arm, starting from your shoulder, then elbow, wrist and fingers. Finally turn your head to look up at your extended hand.

Lower your right arm towards the floor as you exhale, and imagine that you are holding a ball of light in both hands.

As you breathe in visualise raising this ball of light up from the earth as you bring your extended arms up in front of you to shoulder height. Remember to contract your abdominal muscles and keep your right knee bent.

Breathe out as you draw your left arm across in front of you, visualising a beam of light spreading across your chest and turn to face the front. Relax and then lower your arms down to your sides. Repeat on the other side.

modification

Other options include placing your
left hand next to the inner edge of
your right foot or on a block if necessary.

cautions

You should not do this posture during menstruation, pregnancy or for the first
three months after childbirth. If you have back, knee or hip problems, please
be careful whilst performing and holding this posture. The rotated triangle
combines a forward bend and a spinal twist. If you have spinal disc problems
or a hernia, you should avoid this posture. If you have high or low blood
pressure, do not hold the inverted position for long.

...

*a sparkling blue
and white jewel, a light
delicate sky-blue sphere laced
with slowly swirling veils of white,
rising gently like a small pearl in
a thick sea of black mystery*

~ *Edgar Mitchell* ~
(Astronaut)

the earth sequence – prithvi namaskara

Once you have learned this sequence, practise it outside in nature whenever you have the opportunity. This will optimise its benefits.

stage 1

Stand in *tadasana* with your hands interlocked at the level of your navel. Become aware of your breath – feel as if you are breathing all the way down into your lower abdomen.

Inhale and raise your clasped hands – palms facing upwards – in front of your body as far as your throat. Turn your palms to face downwards, and as you slowly exhale, soften your knees and lower your hands back down to your navel. Turn your palms to face forward and, as you inhale, stretch your arms out in front of you and raise them up over your head. Separate your hands and, as you exhale, let them lower gently on either side of your body. Once again, clasp your hands at navel level and repeat this sequence twice.

stage 2

Inhale and raise your hands up to your throat. Exhale, lower your hands and, bending your knees, come down into an 'easy' squatting position (i.e. with your heels off the floor). Turn your palms away from you and bring your hands up in front of you as you stand up on an in-breath. When you have reached full stretch, separate your hands, breathe out and let them slowly come back to the starting position.

Repeat this twice more.

stage 3

Separate your feet to two shoulder widths. Turn your right foot to the right and push your left foot back. Turn your body to the right. Breathe in and, as before, raise your clasped hands to the level of your throat. As you breathe out, lower your hands again, and begin to bend your right knee, keeping your left leg and back straight. When your hands reach the navel, turn them away from you and inhale as you raise your arms up overhead. Unclasp your hands, straightening both legs and visualise a fountain of energy cascading up and out from within you as you lower your arms sideways whilst breathing out. Repeat the sequence twice in this direction, then turn and do it 3 times to the left. Face forward again with feet hip-width apart.

repeat stage 2

repeat stage 1

Return to *tadasana* and close your eyes. Spend a few moments standing still. Allow an awareness of your connection with the earth and every living creature to permeate your whole being. Affirm:

I am one with everything in this entire Universe

mudra of letting go

This is a mudra which will help you to release and let go of any negativity or unwanted thoughts or emotions. You may feel much lighter and freer after holding the gesture for even just a few minutes. The effect of the gesture is amplified when combined with a clear intention to let go of anything which may be blocking your way forward.

Starting with the praying hands mudra, cross your left thumb over your right, extend your index fingers and interlock your remaining fingers over each other.

Sit comfortably and take a few moments to reflect upon whatever it is you wish to let go. Create the mudra and point your index fingers down towards the earth. With every exhalation feel as if the energy which has been locking the pattern into your body is now flowing outwards and down towards the earth.

Release the mudra after a few minutes, place your hands in your lap and spend a few moments breathing in a relaxed way. Now is the time to fill the space you have created with a quality which supports you. With each inhalation focus on replenishing yourself with the positive counterpart to whatever you have released. Affirm:

I am willing to let go of the past, freeing myself to fully embrace the present moment

winter

activation

tadasana into standing meditation

energy block release sequence

pigeon posture

inner fire sequence

deep relaxation

shanti mudra

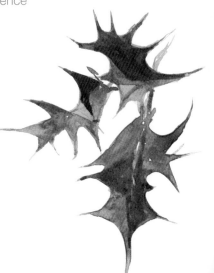

The energy of winter is that of hidden potential and the promise of the future. Although there is not much visible life, it is growing and being nurtured underground, waiting to burst forth. Winter is a time for being still and for nurturing yourself. It is also a time to be introspective and to reflect on the meaning of life and the direction it should take.

A Dru Yoga session designed to support and enhance the energy of winter will focus on building strength and courage, inner and outer. The movements are selected specifically to replenish your resources, allowing you to move fearlessly into the future. Winter is the ideal time to take stock of where you are now and to plan for where you would like to be. Strength and flexibility of the back will enable you to move forward from a point of trust and security.

The pigeon posture provides a strong spinal twist which is excellent for freeing the lower spine. It stimulates the kidneys – the organs located towards the back of the body which are said to propel us forward in life. In the winter they need a lot of energy to counteract the apparent stillness and lack of activity of the season.

The Inner Fire sequence will increase your vitality so that you can move forward into the spring with strength and courage.

The mudra selected for this season, the shanti mudra, is immensely calming and brings a deep sense of peace.

winter tadasana

Tadasana is an excellent posture for meditation. The body becomes still but much is happening just under the surface, in the same way as the earth may appear to be dormant during the winter. As you hold this pose you may experience a powerful build up of energy, usually experienced as heat, especially in the spine.

standing meditation

Adopt the basic mountain posture and allow yourself to settle into stillness, watching the rhythm of your breath.

Focus on a point on the floor approximately two metres in front of you. Relax your upper body, allowing any heaviness in the body to be transferred through the long bones of your legs to your feet and from the feet into the ground.

Visualise a tree firmly rooted into the earth, and experience the same stability as your feet become anchored. Focus on the lower part of your spine and lengthen it upwards. Enjoy the feeling of lightness this creates. Affirm:

In stillness I discover my inner strength

Spend one to two minutes in this posture, remaining still and simply observing whatever sensations arise. Gradually increase the length of time you spend in this standing meditation, building up to ten minutes. You will find it incredibly refreshing and revitalising.

As the weather gets cooler make sure that your body is adequately warmed up before starting the winter programme. The posture and sequence in this section are considerably more challenging than those previously. We suggest you work gently and in stages.

the pigeon – eka pada raja kapotasana

In Dru Yoga we use this variation of the traditional pigeon posture.

1. Kneel in the diamond posture (*vajrasana*).

2. Place your hands on the floor for support and slide your left leg back as far as is comfortable. Place both hands on your right knee.

3. Breathe in, contract your abdominal muscles and raise both arms up in front to shoulder height.

4. Breathe out, twist to your left, keeping your left arm extended with your elbows soft and right arm bent. Keep your gaze at eye level. Relax into this position and take a few breaths.

5. Slowly return to face forward and lower your hands onto your knee. Sit back in the diamond posture once more. Repeat on the other side.

caution

Anyone with hip, knee or lower back problems should perform this posture with care. You may find it more comfortable to place a folded blanket under your knees before starting. You can also do the pigeon posture sitting on a chair.

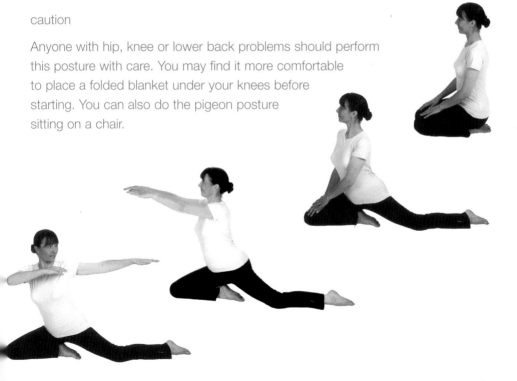

The time has come to turn your heart
into a temple of fire.
Your essence is gold hidden in dust.
To reveal its splendour
you need to burn with the fire of love.

Rumi

the inner fire sequence – agni sarav
stage one – rotated triangle

Stand in *tadasana*. Separate your feet two shoulder widths. Turn your right foot to the right and allow your left heel to lift and move to the left. Still facing forwards, breathe in and raise your arms sideways to shoulder height.

Breathe out and lower your left arm, taking it past your left hip, whilst at the same time turning your body to face the right. As your left arm moves up to shoulder level in front, bring your right hand down towards your right hip.

Breathe in and stretch your left hand forwards. Breathe out, bend forward over your right leg and place your left hand on the floor by the outer edge of your right foot, keeping your knee soft (see autumn rotated triangle posture for modifications).

Breathe normally and take time to feel completely balanced and steady.

Inhale and unfold your right arm like a wing – shoulder, elbow, wrist and fingers. Turn your head to look up at your outstretched arm.

Gently lower your right arm to the floor as you exhale. Look down as you place both hands on the floor on either side of your right foot.

stage two – the runner

Extending your left leg behind you, move into the runner position. Check that your right knee is directly above your ankle and that your left foot is flat on the floor. Breathe in, raise your arms up in front and open them above your head. Breathe out and bend forward over your right thigh, swinging your arms down and behind your back. Repeat this movement twice more and complete the cycle by coming back into the runner position.

stage three – the extended diamond pose

With your right leg still extended, sit back on to your left heel. Bend your right knee and bring your right leg over the left. Hold each foot with your thumb pressing into the sole of your foot. Unfold your right leg and return to the runner position, placing your hands on the floor either side of your right foot. Tuck the toes of your left foot under, straighten your left leg and, taking your weight onto your hands, stretch your right foot back beside your left coming into the inclined plane position.

stage four – the dog

Breathe in, and as you breathe out, walk your hands back,
push your hips into the air and step into the dog posture.
Separate your feet two shoulder widths and hold for a
short while. Breathe in, draw your legs together, and
move into the inclined plane position. Slowly lower
down onto the floor, lowering your knees first.
As you breathe out, bring your arms down
by your sides and relax for
a few moments.

stage five – the bow

Open your knees slightly and bend them, bringing your feet closer to your hips. Take hold of your ankles and, as you breathe in, raise your chest and head up and push away with your legs. Hold for a short while and, as you breathe out, release the hold and lower yourself to the floor. Relax. Repeat this once more.

modification

If the bow posture is difficult for you please replace with the cobra (see page 79).

stage six – the crocodile

Fold your arms, allowing your right hand to hold your left elbow and left hand to hold your right elbow. Rest your head on your forearms. Separate your legs as far as comfortable, with your feet turned out and your heels rolled in. Relax for a few minutes in this position.

When ready, repeat the sequence in reverse order:

Finish by placing your right foot on the floor two to three shoulder widths behind the left foot, as you prepare once more to go into the rotated triangle.

Place your right hand by the outer edge of your left ankle and slowly raise your left arm up into the air, rotating your head to look up. Hold for a short while and then lower your left arm so that both hands are on the floor. Breathe in and raise your extended arms in front of you at shoulder height as you come into an upright position.

Breathe out as you draw your right arm across in front of your chest and turn to face the front. Breathing in, extend your arms at shoulder height and then lower your arms as you breathe out.

Bring your feet closer together and come back into *tadasana*. Stand in stillness for a few moments, absorbing the full impact of the sequence.

shanti mudra

This mudra is different from those for the three previous seasons which were simple hand gestures. It involves the whole body and is done in four stages. As you raise your arms up in front of your body you create a beautiful energetic balance and harmony within your body. The attitude of offering and receiving energy with your arms outstretched above your head instils a sense of inner peace and equanimity.

Stage 1

Sit in a comfortable position, either with your legs crossed or in *padmasana* (lotus posture) and place your hands on your knees with your palms facing up. Bring your hands towards your navel, turning your fingers in towards your body. As you breathe in, bend your elbows and raise your hands upwards to the level of your lower ribs. Hold while you breathe out.

Stage 2

Breathe in and raise up slightly
higher until your little fingers
are level with your sternum.
Palms now face upwards
with fingertips nearly touching.
Pause while you breathe out.

Stage 3

Rotate your palms towards you. Inhale and raise
your hands up to the level of your throat. Hold,
as you exhale.

Stage 4

As you breathe in raise your hands up in front of your
face – mouth, nose, eyes, forehead, and upwards.
As you reach the crown of your head separate your
hands and open your arms out to the sides. Imagine
a shower of golden light cascading from your hands
over your whole body.

Feel this light permeating every cell. Breathe naturally and hold the mudra for a few breaths while affirming:

May Peace fill my heart and may it fill the whole Universe

Once you feel a deep sense of peace settling within you, begin to reverse the movements of the arms, lowering them in four stages, moving as you breathe out, holding still while you breathe in.

a dru yoga lifestyle

your guide to a happy, healthy, balanced life

Yoga practice comes with a positive health warning - change may happen in your life!

As you develop your yoga practice you will start to create harmony and balance within the energetic layers (koshas) of your being. You may find yourself wanting to change your lifestyle as you get more in tune with your own inner yearnings and you become more sensitive to your personal needs. Choices about the food you eat, the type of work you enjoy doing, what exercise suits you best, the people you enjoy being with socially, the kinds of clothes you wear, and so on, may become more intuitive and based on your needs, rather than driven by outside influences.

As you start to integrate yoga into your daily life you may also find yourself searching for more ethical and spiritual principles by which to live. Yoga's wisdom extends beyond the practices of postures and breath control and many of the traditional yoga texts offer guidelines on how to live a good life. In particular, the philosopher/scientist Patanjali, who lived over 2,000 years ago, described a systematic approach to life which had eight elements or 'limbs'. These are all interconnected pathways that lead to enlightenment. They can be likened to the form and nature of a tree.

The limbs are divided into the external:

yama	ethics
niyama	self-discipline
asana	posture practice
pranayama	breath control

and internal limbs:

pratyahara	withdrawal of the senses
dharana	concentration
dhyana	meditation
samadhi	union with the true self

When we start yoga, we usually begin with postures and then move on to breath control and concentration. By working on one limb all the others are encouraged to grow. This is the reason why, when you start to develop your yoga postures, you will find that other parts of your life will be affected.

So, if this is your experience, you may wish to study this chapter to understand the deeper principles of yoga a little more so that you can use them as guidelines for your spiritual journey.

In particular, we will explore the *yamas* and *niyamas* because, combined with *asana* and *pranayama*, they will help you to develop positive attitudes and behaviours towards yourself, those around you and your environment. Once you have been able to integrate these into your life, you will be ready to start on the inner journey of self-discovery and spiritual transformation.

One way of looking at the *yamas* and *niyamas* is to see them offering you the checks and balances that you need to get to your destination in life. The *yamas* are like the brakes of a car. They help you to gain control over your life and restore balance to your body and mind. The *niyamas* are like the accelerator, giving direction and energy. A car without fully functional brakes and accelerator will not get you to your destination and will be dangerous to drive.

yama
ethics, social conduct

The first guideline is *ahimsa*, meaning non-violence, not just to other people but also to yourself and the environment. Vegetarianism is traditionally one of the practices of *ahimsa*, but respecting your health by only eating foods that are good for you and by avoiding anything that may be damaging to your body is a good way of starting. In your yoga practice listen to your body and don't push it beyond what it is capable of doing.

The second *yama* is *satya* or truthfulness. Truthfulness is about being real! It is about seeing things the way they are and it is about getting to know who you are. The more truthful you are, the more you come to know yourself. Being truthful often requires great courage and it should not harm others. If in doubt, stay silent.

Asteya (non-stealing) is the next *yama* and it means not asking for anything you don't need, nor taking what is not yours. When you desire something that does not belong to you, this indicates that you are not content with what you have or who you think you are.

Traditionally the fourth *yama*, *brahmacharya*, was interpreted as chastity, but today we understand it as moderation in all things. Practising self-restraint in all aspects of your life will remind you that over-indulgence and excess is not good for you.

Aparigraha or non-greed is the fifth *yama* and this can also mean non-attachment and non-possessiveness. We often resist change by holding on to things like attitudes, people and possessions in order to feel secure or confident. But it may be that the very things that we are holding onto are preventing us from living our lives with freedom and to the full. Learn to welcome change as an opportunity to grow and move on.

niyama
self discipline, personal conduct

The first *niyama* is *saucha* which means purity or cleanliness. This doesn't only refer to keeping your physical body clean, but also refers to having a pure mind and spirit. Yoga postures can help to cleanse your internal systems but also you need to limit the number of toxins and impurities which you ingest. This includes not only additives and toxins in food and water, but also alcohol and tobacco. These principles should also extend to your surroundings, especially to the place where you practise your yoga.

Santosha (contentment) is the second *niyama*. This is developed by having a positive attitude to everything in your life. Sometimes this is not easy because we are encouraged by advertisements to feel that we are not good enough or don't have enough or don't have the most up-to-date... This fosters such feelings as inadequacy and envy instead of an awareness of the abundance of the world in which we live. Always take opportunities, especially in the stillness after your yoga practice, to appreciate all that you have and all the positive aspects of your life. Appreciation will lead to contentment. Contentment is a choice you make from moment to moment.

The third niyama is *tapasya*, which is traditionally translated as discipline. This may not sound very appealing, but if you wish to succeed at anything you need to work at it. By being creative with your discipline you can be enthusiastic about some of the more mundane aspects of your life. For example, if there are any boring tasks that you need to do, rather than putting them off, just do them and enjoy it. You will find that you become more effective and happy as a result.

Swadhyaya, self-study, is the fourth niyama and it was traditionally based on the study of the yoga texts. Developing self-awareness is a good place to start and this can be experienced as you deepen your yoga practice. As you start to further understand yourself and become aware of the attitudes and behaviours that limit you, you will be able to change them and expand your potential as a human being.

The last of the niyamas is *ishwara-pranidhana* – devotion to a higher being or source of energy. For some people this means worshipping the god of their chosen faith, but for others it may simply be the act of appreciating the awesomeness of nature. Sometimes, when we are really inspired by something we are doing or someone else is doing, we also experience this feeling. Practically, you can work with this principle by expanding your vision of life and then putting your efforts into working towards that vision.

focus on diet

One of the aspects of your lifestyle that you may first want to change is your diet. For thousands of years yogis have followed the same dietary principles – a balance of pure and nutritious food eaten in moderation whilst calm and relaxed. It is important to choose carefully the food that you eat because it becomes a part of you. The coarsest part of the food is eliminated from your body, the less coarse part becomes your flesh. The most subtle part, or the essence of the food, becomes your mind.

Also, pay attention to the food when you eat it. Eat slowly and chew properly.

Unlike western principles of diet which advocate similar diets for everyone, a yogic diet is tailored to the individual's personality, physical build and circumstances. The diet takes account of the principles of *ayurveda* and vegetarianism.

the three doshas

The *ayurvedic* system of health describes three constitutional types or *doshas* – *kapha* (represented mainly by the earth element), *vata* (represented by air) and *pitta* (by fire). Each of us has a constitution which is made up of these three *doshas* in differing proportions, but one always predominates and is reflected in our actions, thoughts and desires. All three *doshas* are also present in food, with one *dosha* again predominating. The balance of our doshas is affected by our lifestyle and diet.

An *ayurvedic* approach to diet aims to balance our *doshas* through the food that we eat. If you can identify which *dosha* is imbalanced, then you can try to balance your energies by eating an appropriate diet, by modifying your lifestyle and by practising specific yoga postures. You need to use your common sense and also take account of the work that you do and the climate and environment in which you live.

When *kapha dosha* is out of balance you tend to feel lethargic, heavy or even depressed. This can be counteracted by reducing the intake of heavy and sweet foods, like bread, potatoes, dairy products, meat and desserts, and by eating less. Try eating lighter foods, like plain rice, steamed vegetables and salads. Spices like ginger and pepper can also activate your system and balance *kapha*.

Unbalanced *pitta* can make you feel agitated, impatient and short tempered. This can be balanced by avoiding hot, stimulating or spicy foods and by eating cooling foods like raw vegetables, fruits and juices, with moderate amounts of lightly spiced heavier foods. Try to eat meals on time or when hungry and avoid too much tea, coffee and alcohol.

When *vata* is out of balance you can feel unfocused, worried and anxious or fearful. You may find yourself rushing about but not achieving very much. Balance this *dosha* by eating regularly, preferably meals which are warm and nourishing such as warm soups, cooked vegetables and moderate amounts of rice or pasta. Drinks should also be warm and taken in moderate amounts between meals.

In general all diets should include wholegrains, pulses, nuts, seeds, fresh and dried fruits, juices, vegetables, herbs, unprocessed sweeteners and dairy products. Ideally they should be fresh, pure and in as natural (organic) a state as possible. These foods are close to nature and still contain a lot of energy from the sun, earth and air. They are also full of *prana* (lifeforce) which creates a lightness, vitality and sense of well-being. This helps to calm and purify the mind and encourages a balanced flow of energy between the mind and the physical body.

a yogic diet

The yogic diet is predominantly vegetarian. Too much meat is heavy to digest, unbalances kapha and can aggravate pitta. It also contains toxins which are difficult to digest and this puts a heavy load on the body's elimination systems.

In general, depending on your constitution, you should eat plenty of fresh vegetables and fruit, some raw and some cooked, and a combination of protein, carbohydrate and fats. Do consider including a good proportion of raw food (complete with their enzymes), fresh juices (which provide a good source of vitamins and minerals) and sprouted foods, which are the most highly nutritious foods available to us.

Grains provide the best form of carbohydrate. Why not try the more unusual ones, like quinoa and millet? It is helpful to reduce the amount of bread that you eat, because it is sticky and heavy and can clog up your digestion. Also, the yeast in bread can unbalance the natural bacteria in the gut, thus reducing the absorption of nutrients. You can get yeast-free sour dough breads made from rye or gluten free flours which are very acceptable substitutes.

It is best to get your protein from nuts, seeds and pulses and foods like tofu, tempeh, tahini, nut butters and hummus, rather than relying on meat and dairy products. If you are working with the principle of *ahimsa*, you may already have started to move towards a vegetarian diet. In the west we tend to eat more protein than we need – even vegetarians!

Dairy products are also a good form of protein, but they can be very mucous-forming, so try to eat them in moderation.

the cleansing effects of water

It is now widely believed that one of the main causes of many of today's common health problems is a chronic state of dehydration. Without water, which accounts for about 80 percent of our body weight, you cannot flush out toxins and regenerate cells. For proper hydration you need to drink plenty of water.

Because of the additives in tap water it's better to drink filtered tap water, rain water or spring water. Your constitutional type will determine how much water you need to drink. If you are *pitta*, your digestion will be strong and your metabolism high, so you can drink plenty of cool water. If your digestion is variable and you tend towards bloating, then moderate amounts of water are better. If, on the other hand, it is slow and strong and you can go for a long time between meals without feeling thirsty, then regular cool or warm water between meals will be good for you.

After your yoga practice, it is especially important to drink water. Doing postures rids the body of toxins and so it is advisable to drink water about fifteen minutes after you finish your practice to facilitate cleansing.

spiritual nutrition

Have you ever wondered why people say 'grace' before eating their meal?
It has been demonstrated using Kirlian photography that food which has
been blessed with a prayer has a much more vibrant energy. Praying over
your food before you eat it will help to energise the food as well as activating
the spiritual layer (*kosha*) of your being. When you pray, you naturally attune to
the still point within you – the point of *Dhruva* – which is linked to the healing
vibrations of the earth and elements. Your healing energy helps to energise
your food.

You may also have noticed that the way in which food is cooked and the
environment in which you eat it, affects your experience of it. Food made in
a calm and relaxed atmosphere is more enjoyable and nourishing than that
made by someone who is angry or stressed – filled with love and care, it
heals and nourishes more than just the body.

Food eaten in a relaxed way is more readily absorbed and often you will
need to eat less in order to feel satisfied because we tend to absorb the
atmosphere in which we eat. As we eat, so we become…

the healing power of nature

In this book we have offered you some very beautiful Dru Yoga sessions, and suggested that you try, as often as possible, to connect with the energy of the seasons by doing your practice outdoors. This is one of the most precious gifts you can give yourself. Not only will you benefit from the increased energy and vitality provided by nature, but you will also experience a greater depth and spirituality in your practice.

If you are not fortunate enough to have access to nature near to your home, then try to take as many opportunities as possible to get out at weekends or on holidays or even during your lunch break. It is important, especially if you are one of those people with a sedentary lifestyle, that you take the opportunity to balance yourself in nature as often as possible. You may be surprised at how much more creative you become. Sometimes decisions are easier to make when you are away from the business and clutter of the every-day world. It is as if all the abundant energy of nature supports you when you allow yourself to re-establish your connection with the natural world.

Walking is one of the simplest, yet most beneficial, forms of exercise and you can also develop it as a form of meditation. Being still in nature, such as sitting silently in the woods or lying face up in a meadow, is to open to its magic, to its sounds, its fragrances, and its seasonal signs. From the promise of spring in the tiniest sprouts of green, to the hint in a swallow's swoop that he has booked his passage, we discover that even long sunny days are numbered.

After the Swallows, what then?

Empty vortexes of air and a swirling desire for freedom
reaching out after their tails following,
like a sadness calling them back to their nests.

But Joy returns like a circle around the woven world,
swiftly streaking sunlight in arcs, golden elipses,
splashing sunshine around like water in an ocean sky.

Swallows, bring a golden smile back to us in glinted eyes,
homecoming eyes, searching for a clean entrance
that your exotic presence may fill with wonder.
You, sleepless on the wing, having dipped your beaks in
and drunk from the depths of an African Sun.

Matthew Wicks

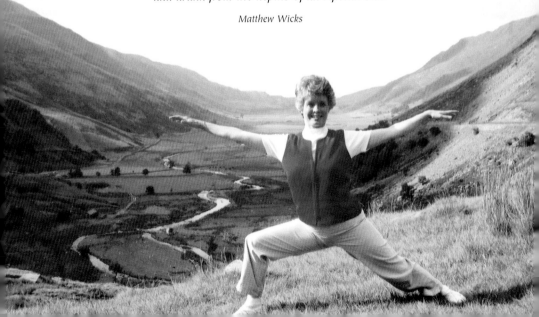

where to go from here

Having experienced the benefits of Dru Yoga from these home programmes, you may be interested in exploring Dru Yoga further. There are many ways in which you can do this.

Firstly, we have produced four CDs to accompany the seasonal practices in the book – one for each home programme. You may find that by listening to the instructions you will be able to practise your yoga with more focus and greater awareness.

Each CD will contain

- activation sequence
- energy block release sequence
- *tadasana* with relevant variations
- a posture
- a Dru sequence
- a relaxation
- a *mudra* to complete the session

You can order these from sales@suryapublishing.com A catalogue
of other Dru Yoga videos, CDs and supporting products is available on
the Dru Yoga website www.druyoga.com

Some of the deeper elements of Dru Yoga can only be fully appreciated
when you learn directly from a teacher. You can do this by joining a class,
by participating in a workshop or by attending a yoga retreat. Information
on where to find a Dru Yoga teacher or class or a local workshop is available
on the Dru Yoga website www.druyoga.com Yoga weekends and longer
retreats are held at the Life Foundation International Course Centre in
Snowdonia, North Wales (enquiries@lifefoundation.org.uk)

If you would like to train as a Dru Yoga teacher, there are branches of the
International School of Dru Yoga in Australia, Canada, Netherlands, Germany,
England, Scotland and Wales. International contact details are available on
www.druyoga.com

concise glossary of sanskrit terms

Agni Sarav	'Honouring the fire within' - a Dru Sequence
Ahimsa	non violence, one of the five yamas
Aparigraha	non possessiveness, non greed, one of the five yamas
Asana	yogic posture
Annamaya kosha	the physical body
Anandamaya kosha	the most subtle layer of our being, the self that sits in the centre of our being where we only experience bliss
Asteya	non-stealing, one of the five yamas
Ayurveda	an ancient model of health and healing
Brahmacharya	self restraint, intelligent control of the senses, one of the five yamas
Chakra	wheel, also refers to one of the 7 power centres of awareness situated along the spine
Dharana	concentration
Dhyana	meditation
Dhruva	permanent and unchanging, the north star
Dhruvakasha	the calm still point we can find within ourselves
Doshas	an ayurvedic categorisation of body types and constitutions
- kapha	a constitution composed of a high proportion of the earth and water elements
- pitta	a constitution composed of a high proportion of the fire and water elements
- vata	a constitution composed of a high proportion of the air element
Eka Pada Raja Kapotasana	the pigeon posture

Hatha yoga	yogic practices pertaining to the physical body
Ishwara-pranidhana	devotion to a higher being or source of energy, one of the five niyamas
Kapha dosha	a constitutional type with a high proportion of earth and water elements
Koshas	five different 'sheaths' or layers of our being
- annamaya kosha	'food' sheath – the most tangible gross layer, the physical body
- pranamaya kosha	the sheath of 'life force', the vital energy layer
- manomaya kosha	the level of feelings and emotions
- vijnamaya kosha	the level of thoughts and ideas
- anandamaya kosha	the sheath where the Self resides
Manomaya kosha	the layer of our existence relating to feelings and emotions
Mudra	a gesture of the body or an attitude of mind
Nadis	energy pathways that prana flows through in the subtle body
Namaste	the praying hands mudra
Niyama	the second of Patanjali's eight limbs of yoga, personal conduct
- saucha	inner and outer cleanliness, purity
- santosha	contentment
- tapasya	self-discipline
- swadhyaya	self-study
- ishwara pranidhana	devotion to a higher being or source of energy
Padmasana	the lotus posture often used for meditation

Parivritta trikonasana	the rotated triangle posture
Patanjali	philosopher/scientist 600 BCE In the yoga sutras,first described a complete process of evolution through yoga
Pitta dosha	constitutional type with a high proportion of the fire and water elements
Prana	life force
Pranamaya kosha	the layer of our being related to our vital force
Pranayama	expansion, control of the life force, breath control
Pratyahara	withdrawal of the senses
Samadhi	state of enlightenment – the final stage of Patanjali's eight limbs of yoga
Santosha	contentment – one of the five niyamas
Satya	truth, one of the five yamas
Saucha	inner and outer cleanliness - one of the five niyamas
Savasana	the corpse posture
Setubandhasana	the bridge posture
Shanti	peace
Surya Namaskara	salutation to the sun – a sequence
Swadhyaya	self-study, one of the five niyamas
Tadasana	the mountain posture
Tapasya	self-discipline, one of the five niyamas
Vajrasana	the thunderbolt posture, also known as the diamond posture
Vata dosha	constitutional type with a high proportion of the air element
Vijnamaya kosha	the level of our being relating to thoughts and ideas
Vinyasa	flow, progression in stages

Vrksasana	the tree posture
Yama	the first of Patanjali's eight limbs of yoga, ethics, social conduct
- ahimsa	non -violence
- satya	truth
- asteya	non-stealing
- brahmacharya	self restraint, intelligent control of the senses
- aparigraha	non possessiveness, non-greed
Yoga	unity

index

acknowledgements

Picture credits

We would like to thank the following people and photographic libraries for their kind permission to reproduce their material. All attempts have been made to trace copyright holders. If any have been overlooked, please contact us and we will rectify it in the next edition.

Janet Baxter p89; Caspar Graham p36,68,125,129; I-stock photo library p14, 44, 49, 58, 134; Life Foundation Photo Library p60, 63, 65, 70, 75, 102, 105, 149, 156, 168, 174, 178, inside front/back cover; Michael Little p25, 28,100; Richard Mulholland p32,109; Jean Napier ARPS p4,15,40,46,73,92,154,164, www.jean-napier.com; NASA p116; Elna Obreen p10; Sam Roberts p18,148; Natasha Seery p166 www.Kirlian-Art.com; Raechel Waters, cover, p85; Lydia Wilson p20; Ilan Shamir poem p74   www.YourTrueNature.com; Matthew Wicks poem p168

Commissioned photography: Photographer: Michael Little Model: Julie Hotchkiss

Clothes supplied by Alice Asquith Illustrations: Joan Groves Proof reader: Catherine Carey

Authors acknowledgements:

The writing of this book has been a joyful experience, made even more inspiring by working with a wonderfully supportive team. Many thanks to Caspar for his friendship and creative design work, to Michael for such fun in his studio, to Julie for her patience and for being a wonderful model, to Joan for contributing her delightful water colours, to Stef for her research, ideas and help with editing, to Catherine for such diligent proof reading, to Keith for advice on diet, to Chris Barrington for supporting us all the way through and to Peter, Jenny, Hazel, John and Raechel for all their help at the end!

It is not customary to acknowledge the trees themselves, though their commitment is total. A tree has been planted and will be cared for to acknowledge that this book could not have been printed without them.

Padma and Helena can be contacted by email at london@lifefoundation.org.uk
or through the Dru Yoga website www.druyoga.com

notes

notes